GOING STRAIGHT

The independent
Unemployment Unit's
guide to jobseekers
leaving custody,
signing on and finding
work

by Martin Blakemore

Published by the
Unemployment Unit

Going straight

The independent Unemployment Unit's guide to jobseekers leaving custody, signing on and finding work

by Martin Blakemore

Published by the Unemployment Unit

322 St John Street, London EC1V 4NT.

British Library Cataloguing in Publication Programme:

A catalogue record for this book is available from the British Library.

ISBN 1-870563-55-7

Designed and printed by RAP Ltd, 201 Spotland Road, Rochdale OL12 7AF

contents

About this booklet

Signing on as unemployed has become more difficult. Major changes have been made in the rights of unemployed people and in what they are expected to do to look for work. This booklet explains what these changes mean for unemployed ex-offenders and those working with them. It explains the benefit rules which apply to ex-offenders who claim the Jobseeker's Allowance (JSA), especially those who want to take up education and training opportunities after their release from custody.

The booklet is divided into five parts:

Part 1 explains the procedures involved in claiming JSA. It covers the 'availability' rules, the 'actively seeking work' test and the 'Jobseeker's Agreement'.

Part 2 describes the various education, training and employment opportunities available to unemployed ex-offenders. In particular, it outlines the detailed eligibility rules that apply to those who wish to access the training and employment programmes offered by the Employment Service and other organisations.

Part 3 describes the complex rules that apply to unemployed claimants who wish to study part-time whilst claiming JSA.

Part 4 offers guidance for education and training providers who wish to provide opportunities for unemployed ex-offenders by explaining how to minimise potential areas of conflict between the courses they offer and the benefit regulations.

Part 5 provides further advice and a list of useful contacts and addresses.

This booklet does not give detailed information on how the amount of JSA a person receives is actually calculated. The focus of the information is on the availability and actively seeking work regulations and how they affect participation in education and training schemes. More detailed information on benefit rates, entitlements and calculations can be obtained directly from the Benefits Agency (BA) or from the publications listed at the end of the booklet.

Abbreviations used in this booklet

To save space, the following abbreviations are used.

ACOP   Association of Chief Officers of Probation

AO   Adjudication Officer

ASW   Actively Seeking Work

BA   Benefits Agency

DfEE   Department for Education & Employment

ES   Employment Service

FEFC   Further Education Funding Council

FEFCW Further Education Funding Council for Wales

IS   Income Support

JSA   Jobseeker's Allowance

LEC   Local Enterprise Company (Scotland)

TEC   Training and Enterprise Council (England & Wales)

TfW   Training for Work

UB   Unemployment Benefit

Sources of information

The information in this booklet is based on official government sources which describe the legal rights and obligations of unemployed people and also the procedures and processes involved in claiming JSA. The legal benefit rules are contained in the 1996 Jobseeker's Regulations which are based on the 1995 Jobseeker's Act. The procedures that the Employment Service should follow when administering benefits are detailed in the JSA Guidance issued to Employment Service staff and Adjudication Officers. Sections of these sources are referred to in the text and full references given at the end of the booklet.

This booklet also uses information published by the Probation Service and voluntary organisations who work with ex-offenders. References to this material are also given at the end of the booklet.

part 1

JSA and ex-offenders: signing on and rights and responsibilities

In 1996 JSA replaced existing benefits for the unemployed. In order to receive JSA you will have to enter into a Jobseeker's Agreement and show that you:

● are available for work,

● are actively seeking work; and

● are capable of work.

There are two types of JSA. If you have paid enough National Insurance contributions while you were previously in work you will be eligible for a non-means tested payment for up to 6 months called 'Contribution-based JSA'.

Most people, however, have to claim 'Income-based JSA' which is means-tested and is calculated in roughly the same way as for those who claim Income Support. An assessment is made of your family circumstances and financial commitments and any savings you have. Even if you only qualify for a small amount of means-tested JSA it means you are automatically eligible for other benefits such as Housing Benefit, free prescriptions, free dental care and so on.

Young persons (YPs) under 18

Most YPs are not entitled to JSA. However, YPs who have just left prison or a young offenders institution are in a 'prescribed group' and may be able to receive JSA for up to 8 weeks. Details of the benefits and training rights of YPs can be found in Youthaid's 'Guide to Training and Benefits for Young People' listed at the end of this booklet.

Availability for Work & Restricted Availability

When you claim JSA you have to show that you are immediately available for 'employment of at least 40 hours per week' and you are expected to be willing to consider any reasonable job that offers more than 24 hours work a week.

Your availability for work can be doubted if you put 'unreasonable' restrictions on the type of work you are seeking. This includes the hours you are prepared to work, the rate of pay you want, and the locality in which you are prepared to work. The key point is that if you limit your availability you generally must be able to show that you have reasonable prospects of obtaining work within the restrictions you impose.

There are certain circumstances where you can place restrictions on your availability and the requirement to be immediately available for work is relaxed if you:

- are engaged in providing a service (paid or unpaid) and are willing and able to take up employment on being given 24 hours notice. NB 'providing a service' applies to those doing Community Service but not those attending Attendance Centres (see below).

- are undertaking voluntary work and are willing and able to take up employment on being given 48 hours notice.

- have caring responsibilities and are willing and able to take up employment on being given 48 hours notice.

- are doing part-time work and are willing and able to take up employment immediately following the statutory period of notice you are required to give your employer.

You may also be allowed to restrict your availability to less than 40 hours per week if you have a physical or mental condition, or you have caring responsibilities, which limits the length of time you can work.[1]

The permitted period & pay levels

When you first sign on you may be given a short 'permitted period' to seek work in your 'usual occupation' which matches the terms and conditions you previously enjoyed. This will last for between one and 13 weeks, depending on your skills, qualifications and experience.

Entitlement to a Permitted Period will be decided by an ES adviser at your first interview. The factors that must be taken into account by the adviser are:[2]

- your usual occupation and any relevant skills or qualifications;

- the length of any training you have done which is relevant to your usual occupation;

- the length of time you have been employed in your usual occupation and the length of time since you were last employed in it;

- the availability and location of vacancies in your usual occupation.

If you have left your usual occupation temporarily it continues to be your usual occupation as long as you have reasonable prospects of finding that employment. At the end of any Permitted Period you are expected to broaden your jobsearch and be prepared to accept a wider range of jobs.

You will not be given a permitted period if you have not got a 'usual occupation', for example, if you have only worked in casual or unskilled jobs.

According to the Chief Executive of the ES "ex-offenders are in fact treated in the same way as any other jobseeker" when determining the length of any permitted period. "This means that each case is looked at on its merits, taking into account any usual occupation, length of time out of the labour market and any vocational training that may have been undertaken."[3]

Please note that if you have been on a full time training or education course for more than two months then you can reject vacancies that are not in the area you qualified for during your first four weeks of unemployment.

Pay levels: the Six Month Rule

In addition to the permitted period you can restrict your jobsearch to jobs which offer your usual rate of pay for up to six months providing that the work you are seeking is not restricted to your usual occupation and you have reasonable prospects of finding work offering your usual rate of pay. After six months you are expected to be more flexible about the pay you will accept.

Good Cause' for refusing a job offer

Outside of the rules above you can be disqualified from receiving JSA for up to six months if you fail to apply for or accept a reasonable offer of employment of 24 hours a week or more. However you may still refuse an offer of work providing that you can show 'good cause' for doing so and providing that the AO accepts that the vacancy or job is unreasonable because:[4]

- the vacancy does not conform to restrictions on availability in your Jobseeker's Agreement;

- it would cause "significant harm" to your health or subject you to "excessive physical or mental strain";

- you have caring responsibilities for someone who is either in your household or a close relative;

- you have a sincerely held religious or conscientious objection;

- it pays on a commission-only basis;

- the travelling time is excessive;

- the work-based expenses you would have to pay (excluding child care costs) would represent an unreasonably high proportion of your wages.

Other factors can be taken into account by the AO when they are deciding whether or not you have "good cause" so you should mention anything that you think is relevant eg problems you might have arranging permanent accommodation.

In most circumstances travelling time of more than an hour in each direction usually counts as "good cause" for refusing a job. Less than an hour may also count if you can show that it would adversely affect your health or is unreasonable because of your caring responsibilities.

Apart from being able to reject a job because the work expenses are too high, you can only turn down a job because of its level of pay if you are covered by the permitted period or six month rule above, or if it pays commission only. You cannot turn down a job just because you think the wages are too low or because it might have an adverse effect on your general household finances. When a minimum wage is set by the Government's Low Pay Commission it will be illegal for employers to pay less than the minimum decided.

What happens if you refuse a job?

If the person who interviews you does not think you have shown good cause for refusing a job they will report your case to a supervisor who will suspend your benefit and refer your case to an AO. You could be disqualified from benefit or have it reduced for up to 26 weeks.

Actively Seeking Employment

If you are signing on as unemployed, you have to show that you are taking 'reasonable steps' to seek work every week. The key principle is that you 'must look in those places where the work that (you) are seeking is likely to be advertised or found; and if opportunities exist, (you) must apply for jobs'.

Legal regulations suggest the following steps you can take:

- oral or written applications for jobs;

- registering with employment agencies and businesses;

- using specialist recruitment procedures; and

- checking in newspapers and magazines.

The steps you take can also include steps to enhance your employability. For example, jobseekers with literacy problems attending a course designed to help with their literacy would be deemed to be enhancing their employability. However, the ES does not consider it "reasonable" for a jobseeker to "continually take steps to improve their employability without ever actually looking, or applying, for a job".[5] You are normally expected to take more than one step each week unless that is all that is reasonable for you to do in that week.

Exceptions to the Availability and Actively Seeking Rules

You are automatically treated as being available for and actively seeking work during the first and last week of your claim. You can also be excused from actively seeking work for a period of up to 2 weeks in any 12 month period because you are away from home. If you intend to be away from home however you must inform the Jobcentre in advance and give them an address where you can be contacted. This is because you must still be available for work whilst you are away. If you are away for longer than 2 weeks you will have to show that you were actively seeking work for the period after the first two weeks.

You can also be excused from being available for and actively seeking work for up to 1 week at a time for a maximum of 4 times in any year in order to deal with domestic emergencies.[6] Please note that if you spend time away from home you are only entitled to means-tested JSA if you remain within the UK.

Availability for Work and Actively Seeking Work for ex-offenders

Claimants who have been discharged from prison or a remand centre are automatically treated as available for work for one week starting from the date of their discharge. A week in this case is a period of seven consecutive days.[7]

Claimants who have been discharged from prison or a remand centre may also be treated as actively seeking employment for up to 8 days from the date of claim depending when their benefit week starts.[8]

The Employment Service has issued guidance regarding the way in which various other circumstances that might apply to ex-offenders affect the availability and actively seeking work requirements.[9]

Bail

According to ES guidance waiting to go to court should not affect a jobseekers availability or prevent them from actively seeking employment.

Court Attendance

Jobseekers who attend court, whether as a witness or as a member of a jury, are not available for employment unless they can show that their attendance will end within 24 hours. This means that you will not be able to claim JSA for the period that you are in court if it is longer than 24 hours.

If you are in receipt of contribution-based JSA you will have to apply to the court for reimbursement of the lost JSA and any expenses involved in attendance at the court. You will need a signed statement from the ES to show to the court to certify that you are currently in receipt of JSA. However, you will have to make a new claim for JSA when attendance at the court ends.

If you are in receipt of income-based JSA you will have to claim Income Support for the period that you are attending the court. You will need a signed statement from the ES to show to the Benefits Agency to certify that you are currently in receipt of JSA. However, you will have to make a new claim for JSA when attendance at the court ends.

Community Service Orders

ES Guidance states that a "jobseeker can be accepted as being available for work while they are carrying out a Community Service order" provided:[10]

(a) they can be notified of a vacancy or interview promptly; and

(b) they are willing and able to rearrange their community service to take up work or attend an interview on being given not less than 24 hours notice.

Your probation officer can help to clarify the flexibility of Community Service programmes to the ES. For example, they can explain that weekend Community Service can be arranged and that Community Service should not be understood to be a barrier to your availability for work.[11] The key availability rule to bear in mind is that claimants must be available for work for a minimum of 40 hours per week.

Attendance Orders

ES Guidance[12] makes clear that "Availability will not normally be in doubt" provided that:

(a) the jobseeker has made arrangements to ensure that notice of a job opportunity or interview would reach them without delay; and

(b) the officer in charge of the centre would release the jobseeker promptly to attend an interview or start a job; and

(c) any further attendances at the centre could be arranged to fit in with any work the jobseeker might get.

Please note that jobseekers attending Attendance Centres are not entitled to 24 hours notice to make themselves available for work because they are not deemed to be providing a service.

Probation Orders

ES Guidance makes clear that "Availability and Actively Seeking Employment is not normally in doubt for jobseekers who have a probation order."[13] As with Community Service Programmes, your probation officer can clarify the flexibility of probation programmes to the ES.[14] For example, if evening programmes can be arranged to fit around your pattern of availability then ask your probation officer to explain this to the ES.

Release Plans

For ex-offenders who are released under licence and required to undertake a course of study as part of their release plan see below in PART III under 'Release Plans'

Temporary Release and Home Leave

Prisoners are not eligible to claim benefits while they are released on temporary licence or on home leave. However if you are staying with someone who is getting income-based JSA or Income Support they can apply to the Social Fund for a Community Care Grant to cover the costs of looking after you while you are at home. More advice is available from the Benefits Agency or the organisations listed at the back of this booklet.

A prisoner on temporary release who claimed JSA would have their claim suspended and referred to the Adjudication Officer (AO) immediately on the grounds that they cannot be regarded as available for work.[15]

Claiming JSA after release from custody and the New Jobseeker Interview

You can contact your nearest Jobcentre by telephone, in writing or in person in order to make an appointment for a New Jobseeker Interview. The first contact that you have with the ES will be with a receptionist. The receptionist's job is to identify your requirements, explain in detail the JSA entitlement conditions, advise you if there is any doubt about entitlement, arrange a New Jobseeker Interview with an adviser and issue a JSA claim pack.

The receptionist should also explain what other information needs to be brought to the interview such as rent books. You will also be expected to provide your National Insurance number. The receptionist should make clear what forms need to be completed before the interview and identify any problems that you might have in completing the forms. ES Advisers can provide help with completing forms, although guidance issued by the Association of Chief Officers of Probation (ACOP) recommends that people under supervision should get impartial advice from a Welfare Benefits Adviser independent of the ES.[16]

Release Papers

Newly released ex-prisoners should try to make sure that they have their release papers with them when they first contact the ES and at the New Jobseeker Interview. This is especially important if they were receiving benefits when they were sentenced and have been released early.

Early Release

Where a newly convicted prisoner was claiming benefits when they were sentenced the ES will have a record of the sentence expiry date. If a claimant has been released early from prison the ES records will therefore show a later date. The ES has systems in place to confirm your early release, however systems can fail and you should take your release documents with you when you first sign on. These can act as proof of identity and show that you have been released early.[17]

Discharge Grants

If you received a discharge grant on release from prison you will need to take your discharge grant form B79(DG) to the interview. If you did not receive a discharge grant you will need to take Form B79. If appropriate, these forms will be used to assess entitlement to Social Fund Payments and Crisis Loans.

The New Jobseeker Interview.

You should make every effort to keep the appointment you have made with the ES. No benefit will be paid until you have attended a New Jobseeker Interview. If missing the appointment is unavoidable you should telephone the Jobcentre to rearrange the appointment.

The interview should take about 20 minutes but times may vary. At the interview the adviser will discuss your previous employment and explain the conditions for receipt of JSA. Help and advice should be given to identify the types of work that you could do as well as advice about job vacancies and training opportunities. Towards the end of the interview a 'Jobseeker's Agreement' (see below) will be discussed and finalised.

Disclosure of convictions

Ex-offenders are under no obligation to declare previous convictions unless asked to do so. However, if you are asked to declare previous convictions, on a job application or at an interview, then it is a criminal offence not to do so, unless, they are 'spent' convictions under the terms of the Rehabilitation of Offenders Act (1974).

The Rehabilitation of Offenders Act (1974) allows some criminal convictions to become 'spent' or disregarded after a set time from the date of conviction. This means that, with certain exceptions, ex-offenders do not normally have to declare these convictions when making job applications. The

Act also makes it an offence for anyone to reveal information about spent convictions to third parties without the full knowledge and permission of the ex-offender.

ES staff are issued with guidance on the Rehabilitation of Offenders Act and can advise you whether your convictions are spent and also whether to tell prospective employers about your convictions.[18]

Detailed advice about how and when to disclose convictions is available from NACRO and the Apex Trust. Addresses and telephone numbers are given at the back of this booklet.

ES staff are told not to help with job applications where ex-offenders refuse to declare unspent convictions when asked to do so on a job application form.

The Jobseeker's Agreement

The Jobseeker's Agreement records three main things; the hours you are available for work each week (known as your 'pattern of availability') any agreed restrictions on your availability and the steps you will take each week in order to find work. No benefit will be paid until a Jobseeker's Agreement has been drawn up and signed by you and the ES adviser.

If you are an ex-offender under the supervision of the Probation Service you can ask the ES Adviser if they will accept jobseeking guidance or assistance organised by the Probation Service as an 'other activity' to be legitimately listed on the Jobseeker's Agreement.

You can also ask the ES Adviser if your Probation Officer can see your Jobseeker's Agreement prior to it being signed. Your Probation Officer might be able to help you to decide what are achievable goals to be written into your Jobseeker's Agreement.

If your Probation Officer thinks that you have unachievable goals in an existing Jobseeker's Agreement then you might be able to amend it following guidance from the Probation Service.[19]

You may have already developed an 'Action Plan' with a voluntary organisation such as APEX Trust designed to help you return to work. The ES Adviser should take this into account when drawing up your Jobseeker's Agreement but will want to ensure that any activities included in your Action Plan offer you the best prospects of finding work.[20]

Although you must have a Jobseeker's Agreement in force in order to receive benefit, this does not mean that the terms of your agreement cannot be changed. If your circumstances change and you feel that the initial agreement is no longer reasonable, you can request that your Jobseeker's Agreement is altered to suit your new circumstances.[21]

Evidence of jobsearch and fortnightly reviews

When you attend the Jobcentre to sign on you may be asked to provide evidence that you have taken the steps described in your Jobseeker's Agreement to find work or improve your employability.

You might be encouraged by the ES to keep a written record of your jobsearch activity and this would count as evidence as well as help you remember what you have done to find work.

Evidence of jobsearch activity should at least match the steps described in your Jobseeker's Agreement and can be in any of the following forms:[22]

(a) evidence in writing from employers, employment agencies, or other bodies which the jobseeker has contacted;

(b) copies of letters the jobseeker has sent to employers;

(c) the jobseeker's uncorroborated written evidence, for example a Jobsearch Activity Log;

(d) the jobseeker's verbal evidence.

If you are an ex-offender under Probation Service supervision and you have difficulty providing evidence, ask the ES if they will accept a note from the Probation Service confirming your jobseeking activity.

The Jobseekers Direction

The Jobseeker's Direction is a new power that has been given to ES advisers which they can use if they consider that you are 'not properly or effectively looking for work'. It enables them to "direct jobseekers to improve their employability through, for example, attending a course to improve jobseeking skills or motivation, or taking steps to present themselves acceptably to employers". It can also be used to instruct someone to follow up specific job adverts or vacancies, or to "register with an employment agency".

If you are issued with a 'direction' you should get advice, especially if you think it is unreasonable. However, while you can appeal against any subsequent sanction you should be aware that failure to comply with a Jobseeker's Direction will result in an immediate two week benefit sanction and failure to comply a second time will result in a four week sanction.

Review Interviews and compulsory courses and programmes

When you have been unemployed and signing on for 13 weeks you will be asked to attend an interview to discuss your jobsearch activities. After each 6 months of unemployment you will have to attend a Restart interview at which your jobseeking activities will be reviewed and changes to your Jobseeker's Agreement will be considered. You have to attend these interviews even if you are taking a part-time course or are involved in other voluntary work.

When you have been unemployed for over a year you will be required to attend one or more compulsory programmes depending on your age at the time of your 12 month Restart interview. If you are aged 18-24, you will be asked to attend a programme of intensive jobsearch counselling interviews called 1-2-1, which may be followed by a four week programme called Workwise (Worklink in Scotland). If you are aged 25 or over you may be referred to either 1-2-1 or a one week 'Jobplan Workshop', or both, at the discretion of the ES adviser dealing with your case. When you have been unemployed for two years you may have to attend either a two week Restart Course or a series of up to seven 'Jobfinder' interviews.

It is important to note that those ex-offenders who are allowed to attend Jobplan Workshops, Restart and Workwise courses as voluntary attenders immediately or shortly after release "will not be subject to sanctions if they fail to attend or complete a programme which they have asked to attend during this period."[23] Sanctions for non-attenders or non completion will only be applied to those who have been unemployed for a year or more and who have been required to attend.

Benefit penalties

If you fail to attend an ES review interview without a good reason your benefit is likely to be stopped. If you fail to sign a Jobseekers Agreement, do not actively seek work, or are not available for work, your benefit is likely to be stopped. You will also be disqualified from JSA if you leave a job voluntarily or through misconduct or if you refuse a 'reasonable' job offer notified to you by the ES.

People who refuse to attend mandatory courses, such as Jobplan Workshops, and prescribed training courses, or who fail to act upon a Jobseeker's Direction" will also be disqualified for two weeks, rising to four if the offence is repeated. This penalty applies to non-attendance on all Government programmes if referral has been through a Jobseeker's Direction.

If your claim for benefit is stopped you should seek independent advice straight away. If you do appeal, make sure that you continue to look for work and sign on as unemployed.

Hardship payments

Hardship payments are available for some people who are sanctioned. The JSA personal allowance is normally reduced by 40%. However, a deduction of 20% applies if the household includes someone who is pregnant or seriously ill.

Please note that there is "no automatic (hardship) payment .. to people who have been sanctioned". Also, hardship payments are not normally available for the first two weeks of the sanction unless you have children; caring responsibilities; are pregnant or have a pregnant partner; or are sick or disabled or have a partner who is sick or disabled. After two weeks, all sanctioned claimants can apply for hardship payments although payment will only be made if someone is judged to be 'suffering hardship'.

Hardship payments are not made automatically. If you wish to claim you have to obtain a JSA hardship application form from your Jobcentre or local Benefits Agency office. You will also need to make an appointment with the JSA Hardship Officer who is normally based at the local BA office.

When you attend an interview you should bring as much evidence of your circumstances as possible, such as birth certificates/Child Benefit books, bank statements, and so on. The BA states that the JSA Hardship Officer 'will normally make their decision on the day' the person applies. If the application is rejected you can appeal against the decision.

The ES/BA provides a short information booklet on the 'Hardship Provision', the JSA9, which should be available in your local office.

Your rights at ES interviews

Many of the ES advisers you see will want to give you the best advice and service they can. However, they also have to enforce the legal regulations and are often under pressure to meet targets and fill schemes.

You are entitled to reasonable treatment and according to the Jobseekers Charter you should be treated politely and courteously at all times. Whilst it will often be necessary to ask direct questions and to be frank on issues of availability and benefit entitlement, interviews should not be conducted in such a way as to attract criticism of harassment or unfair treatment.

You can also bring a 'third party' to a counselling interview. This may be because you need an interpreter; or you may lack confidence and need support; or you might want a witness to the interview. At Restart and other review interviews staff are told that 'objections to a third party should not normally be raised'.

part 2

Education, training and employment opportunities

Employment Service programmes and services

The Employment Service provides a range of programmes and services designed to help people get work. Some are designed to help with jobseeking skills, eg Restart, Job Search Plus and Jobplan Workshop, some provide assistance with finding employment, eg Jobclub and Job Interview Guarantee (JIG), some offer training, eg Training for Work (TfW) and some involve direct work experience eg Work Trials. More details of the programmes and services which are available can usually be found in a leaflet produced by the ES called 'Just the Job'.

During 1997/98, a major New Deal Programme is being introduced for young people aged between 18 and 24 who have been unemployed for over six months. There will be an initial Gateway process of up to four months during which participants will be given job search assistance and advice and guidance. There will also be a range of options available for those who cannot get work immediately. These will all offer training and include either up to six months in a job with an employer (who will be paid a subsidy of £60 a week); six month placements with either a voluntary organisation or with an Environmental Task Force; or self employment assistance. It will also be possible for those who do not have qualifications to study or train full time for up to a year to NVQ level II standard, whilst receiving their benefit payments.

Only young people eligible for JSA will be able to enter the programme, although those with 'special needs', for example, someone with a disability, or who has left Local Authority care in the previous three years, will be able to take up a place from the first day they register for JSA. Time spent in custody will count towards the six month qualifying period.

Eligible young people will be expected to take up a place on the programme and those who fail to do so who do not have a 'good cause' will be subject to JSA benefit sanctions.

'Pathfinder' areas will start to offer the New Deal from January 1998,and offers will be made in the rest of the UK from April 1998. From July 1998 another New Deal programme will be offered to those out of work for over two years. This will involve some employment subsidies and full time education and training opportunities, and more details will be available from the Employment Service, closer to the time.

Relaxed eligibility conditions for ex-offenders

Access to ES programmes usually requires a minimum period of prior unemployment and each programme has its own eligibility rules. In some cases however the eligibility rules can be relaxed for ex-offenders who wish to join these programmes.

For example, in order to join a TfW programme you must normally have been continuously unemployed for a period of at least 26 weeks. However, this qualifying time may have been spent wholly or partially in custody. The rules state that you are eligible to enter TfW if:

you are an unemployed ex-offender and have at least 26 continuous weeks qualifying time made up from time spent in custody, on remand in custody and in continuous unemployment since leaving custody. If you have served all of your 26 week qualifying period in custody, you are not required to have registered as unemployed with the Employment Service.[24]

The following table contains a list of Employment Service programmes and services and shows the normal unemployment qualifying periods[25] and any relaxed eligibility conditions for ex-offenders.

The Chief Executive of the ES has made it clear that these special arrangements "apply equally to those who have been held on remand and not convicted, as well as those sentenced to imprisonment following conviction by a court."[26] He also added that those who choose to attend otherwise compulsory courses on a voluntary basis under those relaxed eligibility conditions "will not be subject to sanctions if they fail to attend or complete" the programme.

Special help from the ES for ex-offenders

Apart from the accelerated entry to some programmes and services the ES considers ex-offenders as a priority group for its 1-2-1 Caseload Interviews. This is a series of up to six interviews with an adviser offering concentrated help with job search and careers guidance. 1-2-1 is compulsory for some claimants after one year of unemployment. However, ex-offenders can join 1-2-1 on a voluntary basis at the New Jobseeker Interview stage, or after 6 months of unemployment.[27]

Programme	Unemployment Qualifying Period	Time Spent in Custody Counts
Restart Course	2 years	yes
Jobfinder's Grant	2 years	yes
Jobmatch	2 years	yes
Jobplan Workshop	12 months	yes
Jobclub	6 months	yes
Job Interview Guarantee	6 months	yes
Work Trials	6 months	yes
Training for Work	6 months	yes
Travel To Interview Scheme	13 weeks	no
Workwise / Worklink (18-24 year olds)	12 months	yes
Job Search Plus	3 months	yes

Training for Work (TfW)

Training for Work (TfW) is the main government sponsored training programme open to unemployed people. It is operated by Training and Enterprise Councils (TECs) in England and Wales and Local Enterprise Companies (LECs) in Scotland. The aim of TfW is to help long-term unemployed people get jobs through training and work experience. Participants in TfW normally receive a £10 per week participation allowance in addition to their usual rate of benefit.

Training programmes supported by the European Commission.

Some probation services, voluntary organisations and colleges provide training courses that are funded by the European Social Fund (ESF). The aim is to improve employment opportunities by providing vocational training schemes and funding job creation measures.

You are eligible to join an ESF-funded project if you are legally present in Britain and if you are coming to the end of, or have completed, a custodial sentence or a period of remand, or have been under restrictive order preventing employment or training, or under a supervision order from the probation service. On completion of the project, any period of custody must have ended so that you are immediately available for work.

Some ESF courses require a prior period of unemployment of 6 or 12 months to qualify however time spent in custody can count towards this qualifying period.[28]

Availability and European Social Fund courses

If a jobseeker has applied for or accepted a place on a course or programme which is wholly or partly funded out of central funds or the European Social Fund (ESF) and which is intended to help a person to select, train for, obtain or retain employment, they can restrict their jobsearch to temporary or casual employment for the period before the course starts.[29] (see below under: 'Training programmes supported by the European Commission').

Special Education and training opportunities for ex-offenders

The National Association for the Care and Resettlement of Offenders (NACRO) organise local employment and training centres, jobclubs, restart courses, job review and jobplan workshops. They also offer a referral service for prisoners wishing to join their programmes upon release as well as pre-employment courses for prisoners nearing release. Their address and telephone number are given at the end of this booklet.

Apex Trust works specifically to improve the employment prospects of offenders and ex-offenders. They run adult training centres, enterprise and self employment projects and jobclubs. Their address and telephone number are given at the end of this booklet.

The Prince's Youth Business Trust aims to help unemployed people aged under 25 to set up their own business and is particularly concerned with helping people under the supervision of the probation service and ex-prisoners. Their address and telephone number are given at the end of this booklet.

The Venture Trust project is based at Applecross in Scotland. The centre runs 20 four week courses each year for a mix of people including young offenders (aged between 16 and 25). The courses aim to motivate young people and to encourage them to make the most of the opportunities on offer. This course is the only one of its kind in the UK where participating Jobseekers are automatically treated as available for and actively seeking employment for the duration of the course. If you get a place on a Venture Trust programme the ES will want to know the dates of attendance on the course and your benefits will then be paid automatically. Further details of the Applecross Venture Trust project are available from probation services.

Further & Higher Education courses

Full time students are not usually entitled to JSA. However, you can continue to claim JSA and enrol on Further and Higher Education courses providing that the course is part-time and providing that you are available for and actively seeking work whilst you are studying. This means that you must be immediately available for work and that you would be willing to give up your course if you were offered a job by the ES.

part 3

Claiming JSA and studying

Unemployed people who are claiming JSA do not have a right to join education or training courses. As an unemployed jobseeker you are only allowed to join courses as a concession and you will only retain your right to JSA so long as you continue to show you meet the following basic rules:

- you are doing a part-time course; and

- you are available to start work immediately; and

- you are willing and able to take time off the course to attend a job interview; and

- you can be contacted promptly while attending the course; and

- you can arrange the hours of the course to fit around a job or you are prepared to abandon your course at once to take up any job of over 24 hours per week; and

- you are actively seeking work.

Obligation to declare involvement and the Student Questionnaire

If you enrol on a course that overlaps with your jobseeking responsibilities you are under a responsibility to inform your local ES office. When you do so you are likely to be issued with a special form - called the ES567S - which asks a series of questions about the course and your intentions. You will have to complete this form but the Chief Executive of the ES has made it clear that you can 'take away the student questionnaire and fill it in, in (your) own time'[30]

The form is designed to test your availability for work and eligibility for benefit. Part 1 has to be completed by everyone who enrols on a course, but if you qualify for 'JSA regulation 11' (see below) and there is no doubt about your availability then you should not have to complete Part 2 of the form.

More detailed information about completing the student questionnaire can be found in the Unemployment Units booklet, 'Studying on the Dole' (details given at the end of this booklet).

Actively Seeking Work & part time courses

Even though a course may lead to qualifications, skills and experience which could help someone obtain work, the ES will not accept course attendance as a 'positive step' towards finding a job and you must continue to follow the steps outlined in your Jobseekers Agreement.

However, it is accepted that you would have less time to look for work whilst attending a course and a Government Minister has accepted that "any time" during which the jobseeker is "participating as a part time student in an employment related course ... shall be taken into account in determining whether the individual has taken sufficient steps to meet the entitlement condition"[31]

Two week employment related course

JSA Regulations provide that attending a full-time job related course for up to two weeks in a year "will be accepted as an active step in seeking employment if it will help improve the jobseeker's chances of getting work". An "employment-related" course means one that helps the individual "gain or enhance the skills needed for employment or seeking employment or a particular occupation."[32]

To be covered by the regulation attendance must be agreed in advance with an ES adviser.

JSA Regulation 11: people who have been receiving benefit for over three months

If you have been unemployed and/or receiving benefit for over three months you may be covered by JSA Regulation 11 which means the course will not of itself be grounds for finding someone unavailable for work.

Regulation 11 stipulates that in determining whether you are available for employment, no matter relating to the course of study shall be relevant providing you are:

- a part time student; and

- willing and able to re-arrange the hours of the course in order to take up employment within your pattern of availability and to take up such employment immediately; and

- have been in receipt of JSA, Incapacity Benefit or IS because they are sick or disabled or has been on a Modern Apprenticeship or Youth Training for a period of 3 months immediately prior to the course starting, or for a total of 3 months out of the previous 6 months if they were working in between.

Please note that "periods in detention are not counted towards the three month qualifying period set out in JSA Regulation 11."[33]

Definition of part-time course

The definition of a part-time course depends on what type of course you want to do, who funds the course and whereabouts in the UK you live.

For Further Education (FE) courses in England and Wales the definition of a part-time course is based on the number of 'Guided Learning Hours' per week. In England these hours are set out in a 'Learning Agreement' signed on behalf of the college and which should be given to you when you enrol on the course. In Wales the hours are set out in a similar document.

For FE courses in Scotland the definition of part-time is more complicated. It is based on the number of hours per week of 'classroom-based or workshop-based programmed learning under the direct guidance of teaching staff' or 'classroom or workshop based programmed learning under the direct guidance of teaching staff which involves additional hours using structured learning packages supported by the teaching staff'[34] The number of hours of your course will be set out in a document like the Learning Agreement signed on behalf of the college.

The 16 Hour Rule and FE courses in Scotland

In England and Wales if the number of 'Guided Learning Hours' per week is 16 or less then it is a part-time course and you can still get JSA if you enrol on it.

In Scotland the number of hours per week of 'classroom-based or workshop-based programmed learning under the direct guidance of teaching staff' must not exceed 16 hours; or where it involves 'additional hours using structured learning packages supported by the teaching staff, the combined total must not exceed 21 hours per week.

The Learning Agreement

ES staff and AOs are told that when considering the situation of individual's under these rules they can only accept as evidence of the number of hours of study a "learning agreement" in England and Wales, and for FE courses in Scotland "a document signed on behalf of the college".

The learning agreement or other document provided by the college should identify:[35]

1. the college;

2. the student;

3. the average number of guided learning hours;

4. the course being undertaken; and

5. if appropriate, the qualification to be achieved.

The document must be signed by the student and someone on behalf of the college, whose position should be stated.

In England and Wales the agreement should also state the weekly guided learning hours of the student or trainee. In Scotland the document should show, the number of hours spent on classroom or workshop-based programmed learning and the number of additional hours using structured learning packages each week.

Other Courses: Higher Education, European Social Fund

The 16 hour rule has been designed to cover FE courses and, according to a Government Minister, does "not apply to higher education and other sectors where the full and part time distinction still exists. In those sectors for many courses the threshold between full and part time courses is 21 hours a week. But that is not always the case. Each case must, therefore, be decided on its own merits. All decisions are made by independent AOs, taking into account the circumstances of each case."[36]

With regard to courses financed by the European Social Fund a Minister has indicated that while the 16 hour rule will be applied to those ESF courses which are provided by FE colleges "there will be no such change for courses that are not funded by the FEFC". For these, "the upper limit will generally continue to be 21 hours per week, with, as now, each case being decided on its merits."[37]

The key principle is that an unemployed person will not be able to take the course if it is described or regarded as full-time.

The decision as to whether a training or education course is deemed part-time or not ultimately rests with the AO. AOs should accept the classification applied to courses by providers 'unless there is strong evidence to the contrary.'[38]

Release Plans and part-time education or training courses

Where release plans require a person to undertake a course of study they will be eligible to receive JSA providing that the course is part-time and providing that they still meet the availability and actively seeking work conditions. A government Minister stated that "effective liaison between the ES and the Probation Service is important. ES needs to be aware of the obligations of the prisoner released on probation and the Probation Service needs to understand the entitlement conditions for unemployment benefits, including re-arranging a course if the person receives an offer of employment."[39]

Access courses and availability

Some unemployed people have had their benefit stopped while participating in Access courses. Colleges have been told that access courses which are linked to entry to higher education or to specific occupational outcomes mean that the individual concerned cannot be available for work. When the point was put to a Government Minister he made clear that "unemployed people can take access courses while claiming unemployment benefits, so long as the course is part time and they remain available for and actively seeking employment."[40]

Evening classes, open learning and availability

If you are studying in the evening your availability for work is not affected unless the jobs you are seeking require you to work during the hours of attendance on the course, for example bar work which involves evening shifts. However the course must be part time.

If you are participating in an open learning programme and are studying at home in your own time then benefit can continue so long as you remain available for and actively seeking employment.

'Signing On' and part-time study or training

The local ES office has discretion about when to require a claimant to sign on if they are participating in a part-time course. According to a Government Minister "local office managers are encouraged to vary signing times and/or days to facilitate clients undertaking a course of study or training, providing they are satisfied attendance does not prevent an individual from fulfilling the conditions for receipt of benefit".[41]

ES staff are told that, if you state that you "are unable to attend (to sign on) on the allotted day or time due to (your) part time study, (they should) make alternative attendance arrangements".[42]

Compulsory Government programmes and part-time education and training courses

In an earlier section it was explained that if you have been out of work for a long time you will be required to attend a variety of compulsory Government programmes, ranging from Jobplan Workshops to Restart Courses. This requirement will apply even if you are involved in a part-time course. However, a Government Minister has indicated that "wherever possible arrangements will be made for attendance to fall at a time outside normal study hours or exam times."[43]

When a claimant attends the Jobplan Workshop or Workwise or Restart Course they may want to get the course or workshop leader to include their part-time course in any Action Plan they develop.

part 4

Information for education and training providers and others working with ex-offenders

In order to maximise opportunities for unemployed ex-offenders, education and training providers need to be aware of ways in which they can minimise potential areas of conflict between the courses and programmes they offer and the benefit regulations.

Preceding sections give a detailed guide to the JSA regulations and the conditions for receiving benefit whilst studying or training. Long term further education is often seen by the Probation Service as an integral element of a course of action which is designed to reduce offending. However to enable ex-offenders to participate in part-time courses it is vital that they do so in conformity with the rules outlined in this booklet. Effective liaison between the various agencies involved, such as that provided through local offender employment forums, is important to promote greater involvement in available courses.

Part-time training and education courses

If a claimant is deemed to be a full-time student, or if the course they are taking is deemed to be a full-time course they will not be entitled to JSA. Courses must be deemed part-time by the ES and claimants will need to provide clear evidence that they are.

Course descriptions and prospectuses should be clear regarding the part-time status of the course and should not be compromised by other written material e.g. a full-time course within the same prospectus offering the same course material or qualification over the same length of time.

College course co-ordinators and training providers can help by being flexible and imaginative with regard to the structure of courses and the mix of learning modes employed on the courses they offer.

Training programmes supported by the European Commission

Project funding is available to probation services and voluntary organisations from the European Social Fund (ESF) for employment and training purposes. The aim is to improve employment opportunities by providing financial support for the running costs of vocational training schemes and job creation measures. Applications for funding should be made to the DfEE although local authorities often organise schemes.

Please note that participants on ESF courses can only continue to receive JSA if the course is part time and they show they are available for and actively seeking employment.

Probation Services

Effective liaison between probation services and the ES can help to ensure that probation programmes do not jeopardise benefit entitlement. Probation officers can explain to the ES how the obligations of ex-offenders released on probation can contribute to their employability rather than being seen as a barrier to finding work. The following advice is taken from ACOP Advice on Employment, Training and Education Issues (1994).[44]

Community Service:

Community Service can contribute to improving offenders' employment prospects, particularly if:

- The C.S. placement takes account of the offender's employment or training need;

- assessment and exit interviews include work on employment prospects; and

- consideration is given to linking Community Service to the NVQ framework.

Probation Centres:

Probation Centres can also make a valuable contribution to improving offenders' employment prospects. Possibilities include:

- ensuring that groupwork and individual counselling addresses employment issues (i.e. assessment; information and advice; motivation and referral);

- considering how the probation centre programme can complement mainstream training and employment preparation programmes; and

- considering how offenders attending probation centres might access appropriate NVQs.

Action Plans

Action plans drawn up for individual claimants by organisations other than the ES need to take account of the JSA regulations and entitlement conditions. ES staff are encouraged to transfer activities from action plans onto Jobseeker's Agreements and are issued with the following guidance when considering action plans already drawn up by outside organisations:45

"If someone presents an action plan at a new jobseeker interview, take it into account when discussing the Jobseeker's Agreement. If appropriate, transfer activities from it into the Jobseeker's Agreement. Remember, however, that:

(a) an action plan agreed with a voluntary organisation is unlikely to be purely focused on getting the jobseeker back into work and may include a number of non-work related activities; and

(b) the Jobseeker's Agreement must, if followed, offer the jobseeker the best chance of success and satisfy the JSA labour market entitlement conditions. It must not be compromised by any activities agreed between the jobseeker and the voluntary organisation."

going straight

part 5

Further sources of advice and information

Citizen's Advice Bureaux (CAB)

Local CAB telephone numbers should be in the phone book. The National Association of Citizens Advice Bureaux (NACAB) will be able to tell you where your nearest CAB is located. Tel: 0171 833 2181.

Advice Centres

The Federation of Independent Advice Centres can tell you where its local advice centres are located. Tel: 0171 274 1839

Law Centres

Some Law Centres have welfare rights workers. To find out if there is a law centre in your area call the Law Centres Federation. Tel: 0171 387 8570

NACRO

The National Association for the Care and Resettlement of Offenders is the largest voluntary organisation concerned with promoting the care and resettlement of offenders. NACRO run a wide range of services including employment and training centres, Jobclubs, restart courses, job review and jobplan workshops. They also produce free leaflets about 'Disclosing Convictions', the 'Rehabilitation of Offenders Act 1974' and 'Criminal Record Checks'. NACRO's head office is at 169 Clapham Rd, London, SW9 0PU. Tel: 0171 582 6500

Apex Trust

Apex Trust is a voluntary organisation working to improve the employment prospects of offenders and ex-offenders. Apex Trust run a range of services including adult training centres, self-employment projects and Jobclubs. They produce a guide called 'Straight for Work' which gives detailed advice on why how and when to give information about criminal records to employers which costs £2.90 incl p&p available from; Apex Trust, St Alphage House, Wingate Annexe, 2, Fore Street, London, EC2Y 5DA. Tel: 0171 638 5931

Employment Service (ES)
A booklet available from the ES at your local Jobcentre called 'Just for the Record' (OFJI) gives information about disclosing convictions to employers.

The Prince's Youth Business Trust
A charity which is particularly concerned to help young people under probation service supervision set up their own business. Tel: 0171 925 2900.

The Unemployment Unit booklet: 'Signing on for Jobseeker's Allowance' (September 1996)
Gives more details about your rights and the procedures involved in claiming JSA. It details the signing process and how a claimant's jobseeking activities will be reviewed and what their rights are and costs £2.00 Available free to claimants or trainees who send an A5 sized stamped (31p) addressed envelope to the Unemployment Unit.

The Unemployment Unit booklet: 'Studying on the Dole'
Provides more information on the JSA rules for studying or training part-time. Cost £2.00 Available free to claimants or trainees who send an A5 sized stamped (31p) addressed envelope to the Unemployment Unit.

The Unemployment and Training Rights Handbook (421 pages, 5th edition 1997)
Contains highly detailed information and is available from the Unemployment Unit at £9.95.

Youthaid's 'Guide to Training and Benefits for Young People' (142 pages, revised edition 1996)
Costs £6.95 and is also available from the Unemployment Unit at 322 St John Street, London, EC1V 4NT.

Up to date information on government schemes, benefits and allowances, new Employment Service procedures and legislation is given in the Unemployment Unit's monthly journal 'Working Brief' which is available on subscription. For details, write to the Unemployment Unit.

CPAG
The Child Poverty Action Group produce a range of welfare benefits handbooks and advice guides. CPAG are at 1-5 Bath Street, London EC1V 9PY. Tel: 0171 490 0561

References

To save space, the following abbreviations are used for references to the benefit regulations and the internal Employment Service JSA guidance:

Association of Chief Officers of Probation, Employment Working Group
ACOP EWG

Jobseeker's Allowance Regulations
JSA Regs

JSA Guidance "Interviewing Policy" volume
JSA (IP)

JSA Guidance "Interventions" volume
JSA (Int)

JSA Guidance "Jobseeker's with Special Needs" volume
JSA (JSN)

JSA Guidance "Local Office Adjudication" volume
JSA (LOA)

JSA Guidance "New Jobseeker Interviews" volume
JSA (NJI)

JSA Guidance "Product Knowledge" volume
JSA (PK)

Employment Service Adjudication Officer's Guidance
AOG

TEC & CCTE Planning Prospectus Requirements & Guidance 1997-98
TEC (PP)

1. JSA Regs, regulations 13(3)&(4)

2. JSA (NJI), chapter 3, paragraph 93

3. Letter to C. Short MP from L. Lewis, Chief Executive of the ES, 9/4/97.

4. JSA Regs, Regulation 72(2)

5. JSA (LOA), chapter 2, paragraph 310(b)

6. JSA (LOA), chapter 2, paragraph 116

7. JSA (LOA), chapter 2, paragraph 100

8. JSA (LOA), chapter 2, paragraphs 101,102

9. JSA (JSN), chapter 5, paragraphs 31-39

10. JSA (LOA), chapter 2, paragraph 338

11. ACOP (EWG), Job Seeker's Allowance Guidance, August 1996, p.2

12. JSA (LOA), chapter 2, paragraph 341

13. JSA (JSN), chapter 5, paragraph 37

14. ACOP (EWG), Job Seeker's Allowance Guidance, August 1996, p.2

15. JSA (LOA), chapter 2, paragraph 277

16. ACOP EWG, Job Seeker's Allowance Guidance, August 1996, p.4.

17. JSA (Int), chapter 24, paragraph 18(b)

18. JSA (JSN), chapter 5

19. ACOP (EWG), p.4

20. JSA (IP), chapter 4, paragraph 30

21. JSA (LOA), chapter 4, paragraph 35(e)

22. JSA (LOA), chapter 2, paragraph 302

23. Letter to C. Short MP from L. Lewis, Chief Executive of the ES, 9/4/97.

24. TEC (PP), paragraph D29.1 & annex B.

25. JSA (PK), chapter 30.

26. Letter to C. Short MP from L. Lewis, Chief Executive of the ES, 9/4/97.

27. Letter to C. Short MP from M. Fogden, Chief Executive, of the ES, 28/2/96 and JSA (Int), Chapter 16, paragraph 7

28. ESF Unit, DfEE, 1996: Guidance for 1996 Applications.

29. JSA (LOA), chapter 2, paragraph 318

30. Letter to T. Rooney MP from M. Fogden, Chief Executive of the ES, 11/12/96).

31. Hansard Written Answers, col 41, 4/3/96.

32. AOG, vol 6, para 35030, 1996.

33. Letter to C. Short MP from L. Lewis, Chief Executive of the ES, 9/4/97.

34. JSA (LOA) chapter 3 paragraph 9(b)

35. AOG, vol 6, para 35029, 1996:

36. Letter to T. Rooney MP from E. Forth, Minister of State, DfEE, 21/9/95.

37. Hansard Written Answers, col. 476, 25/4/95.

38. JSA (LOA) Chapter 3, paragraph 29

39. Letter to T. Rooney MP from E. Forth MP, Minister of State DfEE, 21/9/95

40. Letter to T. Rooney MP from E. Forth, Minister of State, DfEE, 21/9/95.

41. Hansard Written Answers, col 244, 22/3/95.

42. JSA (Int), chapter 6, paragraph 35.

43. Hansard Written Answers, col 246, 22/3/95.

44. ACOP, Employment Working Group, April 1994, pp.9-10.

45. JSA (IP), chapter 4, paragraph 30(a)&(b)